A Class Act Production

THE ELVES
AND THE SHOEMAKER

CW00448953

A Magical Christmas Musical

by

Sara Ridgley & Gavin Mole

IMPORTANT NOTE TO THE PRODUCER
A reasonable licence fee is payable if you wish to perform this work in public.
Please see the application form at the back of this book for details and for information on your free Publicity Pack.
Please note: Blanket performance licences issued by the PRS or any other establishments *DO NOT* cover this work.

Editor: Louisa Wallace

Music processed by: Writers of Note! Limited

Cover Design: Glide Design

CD: Arranged and produced by Gavin Mole and Peter James, sequenced by Peter James
Engineered and mixed by Damon Sawyer at The Park Studios, Bracknell
Saxophone by Alan Whetton
Executive producers Sara Ridgley and Gavin Mole

Published 2001

International
MUSIC
Publications

This book has been produced with special regard to the environment. We have insisted on the use of acid-free, neutralized paper made from pulps which have not been elemental bleached and have sought assurance that the pulp is formed from sustainable forests.

ACKNOWLEDGEMENTS
Sara and Gavin wish to express their gratitude to Cheron Mole for her support and patience; to Peter James and Damon Sawyer for musical wizardry in the studio and to the Class Act Productions Gang for their performance on the recording.

This musical is dedicated to Sue Dadley of St Joseph's School, Coventry for her commitment to music theatre in education and to Sue and the pupils of St Joseph's for their spectacular performances of our work.

CONTENTS

INTRODUCTION

Welcome to **CLASS ACT PRODUCTIONS**, a series of easy-to-stage musicals by Sara Ridgley and Gavin Mole, creators of the *Box Office Productions* series of 'Around The World' musicals and *Sing It & Say It (Can Anyone Play It?)*, also available from IMP.

CLASS ACT PRODUCTIONS are based on well-loved traditional tales, told through original lyrics and lively music to help you present a complete theatrical experience for the whole school.

FEATURES
❋ Suitable for children aged 4 to 7
❋ Minimum cast size: 30
❋ Performance length: c30 minutes
❋ Singing and non-singing solos
❋ Simple percussion parts
❋ 'Join-in' story for audience participation

PACK INCLUDES
❋ Piano score with guitar chords
❋ Performance CD (backing track with and without vocals)
❋ Script with stage directions (photocopiable on payment of performance licence fee)
❋ Publicity Pack (will be sent free of charge on receipt of performance licence fee)

PRODUCTION PAGES
❋ Who Plays Who? (User-friendly Cast List)
❋ Who Sings What? (Rehearsal Planner of who takes part in each musical number)
❋ Who Plays What? (Percussion Chart)
❋ Who Wears What? (Costumes Chart)
❋ Who Carries What? (Essential Props List)
❋ What's It Going To Look Like? (Staging/Scenery/Lighting suggestions)
❋ Who Goes Where? (Movement/Dance ideas)
❋ Who Does What? (Business/Fundraising plan - not compulsory!)
❋ Who's Done What? (The Final Countdown – a checklist for opening night ...)

WHO PLAYS WHO?
(Cast List)

CHARACTER	DESCRIPTION	ACTOR
Stefan Sole	A good man on hard times (but he's still singing)	
Sue Sole	Stefan's sweet-singing, business-minded 'solemate'	
Toecap	A big-voiced town crier who moves the tale along and keeps order	
Mutter	One of Toecap's dozy apprentices, with simple minimal lines	
Mumble	Apprentice number two. Mutter's never seen without Mumble	
Benjamin	Mr Candelabra, skilled maker of candles and candlesticks	
Barbara	Benjamin's bossy wife	
Donald Rump	A singing millionaire beef rancher from the state of Texas	
Philly Meenyon	Donald's eyelash-fluttering, credit card-wielding lady	
Sesame Seed	Kindly Master Baker of the village of Leather Uppers	
Poppy Seed	Sesame's industrious, strudel-baking wife	
Darlene Deep	A tough, rich Australian opal mine owner	
Doug Deep	Darlene's husband, an 'outback' man of very few words	
Slingback	A 'heel' of a property developer with evil intentions	
Bootlick	One of Slingback's cowardly bailiffs	
Footpad	Bootlick's fellow henchman, a trainee bully	
Magigayle	A good fairy, keeping Elves and audience in order	
Flipflop	Lazy foreman, supervising from behind his newspaper	
1st Elf	Real Elf Leader with solo spoken lines and group songs	
2nd Elf	Can never find his pins but he's a hard worker	
3rd Elf	An industrious Elf who likes to produce perfect stitches	
4th Elf	A sensible Elf with 'chunky' lines to chant and sing	
5th Elf	A streetwise Elf with a market trader's sales talent	
6th Elf	An Elf with a military attitude to his work	
Serena Stiletto	A little rich girl with showbiz aspirations	
Instep	Serena's silent, mysterious bodyguard and manservant	
Naughty Boy	He misbehaves – until Toecap sees him (non-speaking)	
Naughty Girl	Mischievous sister to Naughty Boy (non-speaking)	
Grandma	She's watching you, Naughty Boy (non-speaking)	
Grandpa	Ability to snooze in a chair required. Er, Headmaster?	
Narrator 1	Chosen from the Ensemble to lead the 'join-in' story	
Narrator 2	A key part of the warm-up act	
Narrator 3	Encouraging the audience to put their 'sole' into it (sorry!)	
Narrator 4	Helping the audience lose their inhibitions	

ENSEMBLES

Ensemble	Maximum numbers for the maximum volume (divided into Group 1 and Group 2)	
Descant Singers	A group to add top notes to the opening number (could double as The Kitten Heels)	
Candelabra children	Five non-speaking parts, ideal for smaller children (but requiring a degree of manual dexterity!)	
Seed children	Five more small roles (with no solo lines to learn), but needing simple physical co-ordination	
Royal party	Ensemble members who become Stefan's rich and royal customers	
The Kitten Heels	Serena Stiletto's backing singers (bluesy soul-singing ability and cool 'attitude' required)	

WHO SINGS WHAT?
(Rehearsal Planner)

CHARACTER → / SONG ↓	Ensemble	Toecap	Mutter & Mumble	Stefan	Sue	Benny Barbara Poppy Sesame	Donald Philly Doug Darlene	Slingback Bootlick & Footpad	Magigayle	Flipflop & The Elves	Serena & The Kitten Heels
It's Holiday Time!	✔	✔									
Toecap's Talking		✔	✔			✔	✔				
Shoes		✔		✔							
Sue's Lament				✔	✔						
Raising Your Rent				✔				✔			
Sue's Lament (Rep)					✔						
Elves Rap									✔	✔	
Magigayle's Mus Spell									✔	✔	
Morning's Dawning				✔	✔						
Serena Stiletto											✔
Lucky Day	✔			✔	✔						
Elves Rap Again									✔	✔	
Magigayle's Spell (Rep)									✔	✔	
Buy, Buy, Buy!				✔	✔		✔				
Toecap's Talking Shoes		✔	✔	✔	✔						
Elves Rap Again (Rep)									✔	✔	
When Someone's Kind	✔			✔	✔					✔	
It's Holiday Time (Fin)	✔	✔	✔	✔	✔	✔	✔	✔	✔	✔	✔
Bows	✔	✔	✔	✔	✔	✔	✔	✔	✔	✔	✔
When Someone's (Rep)	✔	✔	✔	✔	✔	✔	✔	✔	✔	✔	✔

❋ For the easiest way to learn the songs, we recommend that you listen to the performance on the CD with the children, then teach them the words, ideally by rote, but if they want their own scripts, feel free to photocopy as paying the licence fee covers all the copyright legalities for you.

❋ 'ENSEMBLE' parts are for your designated Ensemble singers. 'ALL' means every cast member sings (even if they're offstage). 'EVERYONE' means the audience joins in, too.

WHO PLAYS WHAT?

(Percussion Chart)

Feel free to add your own percussion!

INSTRUMENT ▶ SONG ▼	Bells	Gong	Triangle
It's Holiday Time!	✔		
Shoes		✔	
Sue's Lament (Reprise)			✔
Magigayle's Musical Spell			✔
Lucky Day			✔
Magigayle's Musical Spell (Reprise)			✔
Toecap's Talking Shoes		✔	✔
When Someone's Kind			✔
It's Holiday Time (Finale)	✔		
Bows		✔	

WHO WEARS WHAT?
(Costumes Chart)

CHARACTER	COSTUME	COMPLETE?
Stefan Sole	Old clothes, worn leather waistcoat, tool-belt, half glasses	
Sue Sole	Patched skirt, a blouse that's seen better days, apron	
Toecap	Breeches, buckle shoes, white shirt, grand coat, tricorn hat	
Mutter	Breeches and page-boy tabard to match Toecap's costume	
Mumble	As Mutter (he's too lazy to think up a different outfit)	
Candelabras	Work smocks or overalls with pockets for tools of the trade	
Donald Rump	Smart suit, tie and stetson (all in white?), cowboy boots	
Philly Meenyon	'Dallas'-style outfit, expensive but over-the-top, big hair	
Seeds	Chef's checked trousers, large white aprons, chef's hats	
Darlene Deep	Designer dungarees? Bushwear? She's a grown-up tomboy	
Doug Deep	Bushwear, possibly big khaki shorts on little legs?	
Slingback	Black cloak or sharp suit, black shirt, white tie, fedora	
Bootlick	Black leather jacket, black trousers with cool shades	
Footpad	As Bootlick (he wants to look like a real tough guy)	
Magigayle	Sparkly dress, ballet shoes, tinsel garland in her hair	
Flipflop	Brown foreman's overalls or T-shirt saying 'BOSS'	
Elves	Ragged shirts, scruffy trousers, bare feet, torn hats	
Serena Stiletto	Glittery cabaret-singer dress, long gloves, sparkly shoes	
The Kitten Heels	Matching evening dresses (as long as they don't outshine Serena!)	
Instep	Black roll-neck sweater, jacket and trousers, sharp shades	
Kings and Queens	Grand robes, rich velvet cloaks, jewelled crowns	
Ensemble	Colourful winter clothes for sledging and skating on the lake	

WHO CARRIES WHAT?
(Props List)

PROP	CHARACTER	SONG	✔
Walking stick	Grandpa	It's Holiday Time!	
Handbell	Mutter *(for Toecap)*	Toecap's Talking	
Tricorn hat	Mumble *(for Toecap)*	Toecap's Talking	
Two menorrah with candles	Benny and Barbara	Toecap's Talking	
Two candles	Candelabra children	Toecap's Talking	
Large wallet of credit cards	Donald Rump	Toecap's Talking	
Handbag	Philly Meenyon	Toecap's Talking	
Two trays of pastries	Sesame and Poppy	Toecap's Talking	
Two sugar shakers	Seed children	Toecap's Talking	
Leather pieces and tools	Stefan	Shoes	
Embroidered jacket and hat	An assistant *(for Stefan)*	Shoes	
Torch	Stefan	Sue's Lament	
Sparkly wand	Magigayle	Elves Rap	
Newspaper/journal	Flipflop	Elves Rap	
Bankroll	Instep	Serena Stiletto	
One pair red high-heeled shoes	Instep *(from Sue for Serena)*	Serena Stiletto	
Two pairs of shoes	Stefan	Buy, Buy, Buy!	
Six sets of clothing and boots	Elves	When Someone's Kind	

WHAT'S IT GOING TO LOOK LIKE?
(Staging/Scenery/Lighting)

THE ELVES AND THE SHOEMAKER can be performed with snowy simplicity or Broadway glitz – it's up to you – but time, budgets and facilities allowing, here are some straightforward ideas to help to create a memorable music theatre experience.

SCENERY

❄ It's deepest winter in the mountain village of Leather Uppers (icicles on signpost?) Paint a Christmas-card snowy backdrop of white card mountains.

❄ Place a decorated Christmas tree upstage centre. Use two other firs in pots, decorated with spray snow, downstage left and right. Alternately, glue cut-out trees silhouetted on your cut-out mountains!

❄ Stick paper doyley snowflakes on stage curtains and hang them on threads from the roof above the stage and audience. Try a snowy curtain of floaty fabric hung across backstage, an acetate of a downloaded internet image back-projected, a transparency through a slide projector (or pure imagination). Cross your fingers for real snow!

❄ Simple cardboard 'shop-fronts' for the Candelabras and Seeds.

❄ Use an old trestle table as a workbench to represent Stefan's workroom and a simple shop window for him to display his shoes.

❄ Set two chairs for Grandma and Grandpa for the opening number, then take one off so Flipflop can use the remaining one when he's 'supervising' from **ELVES RAP** onwards.

STAGING

❄ Lift the action with stage boxes. It not only gives the audience a better view, but adds to the sense of venue, occasion and performance for the company.

❄ A stage with an 'apron' area is ideal for characters to perform downstage from Ensemble scenes (use it as a 'catwalk' during the Shoe Parade in **SHOES**; for the isolation of **SUE'S LAMENT** and as a nightclub-style stage for **SERENA STILETTO**).

❄ Find onstage places for the Elves to hide (behind the shop-fronts is ideal).

❄ Perform in the round if you have the facilities to make several stage areas.

LIGHTING

❄ Bright winter's daylight for the first three numbers then a darker state for **SUE'S LAMENT** and **RAISING YOUR RENT**.

❄ Stefan can use a torch to lock up during **SUE'S LAMENT** (candles are great, but ...)

❄ If safe, go to blackout for **ELVES RAP**, ideally with white Christmas lights switched on and off to match the musical 'sparkles', then a bright state after **MAGIGAYLE'S MUSICAL SPELL** has worked and the Elves can be seen (happens three times).

❄ A gradual increase for **MORNING'S DAWNING** is effective.

❄ A bright state for **SERENA STILETTO** (or 'nightclub' lighting if you prefer).

WHO GOES WHERE?
(Movement/Dance)

❇ Use the 'join-in' story printed in your programme for the audience to, er, join in with. Either bring your four Narrators on down through the audience, talking as they walk and getting the audience involved, or have them run onstage. Bang a gong or cymbal to silence the audience first. Find the smallest child and the biggest gong, then ask them to stand centre stage with a perfectly straight face and hit it, big time!

❇ The show opens on a deserted stage. One child runs on alone, followed by excited crowds until the entire Ensemble is onstage. Keep them onstage throughout if there's enough space to act out the smaller scenes in front of them. They can help the audience with *MAGIGAYLE'S MUSICAL SPELL* and join in with the Elves' lines 'all night' and 'all day, workin' all night, workin' all'.

❇ *IT'S HOLIDAY TIME!* will inspire 'knees-bend-skating-standing-still' movements (listen to the CD and all will become clear) then a more rocky feel to the movement. The children will have great dance ideas, guaranteed.

❇ The royal party fantasy sequence and Shoe Parade of Stefan's number, *SHOES*, should be a whirl of movement from the VIPs and Stefan's staff showing off his shoe designs along a cat-walk. The royal party stage a regal return for *TOECAP'S TALKING SHOES*.

❇ Bootlick and Footpad will find finger-clicking moves for *RAISING YOUR RENT*.

❇ The Elves use lots of over-exaggerated sewing movements during their scenes (use giant cardboard sewing needles, cotton reels and buttons) to contrast with immobile, lazy Flipflop. Choreograph a heel-toe and clapping dance routine for their final scene when they're celebrating their new clothes.

❇ Magigayle can berate the audience with some balletic sparkling up and down the aisle for her spell, if it's practical. Just watch the sharp points on that wand.

❇ Serena Stiletto and The Kitten Heels will start choreographing their own dance routine for their scene as soon as they hear their music. Naturally, the staff should learn this as well (for the Christmas party!)

❇ During the *BOWS*, Ensemble take a bow, then the cast walk down in this order:
  - ❇ Mutter and Mumble
  - ❇ Candelabra family followed by Donald and Philly
  - ❇ Seed family followed by Doug and Darlene
  - ❇ Royal party
  - ❇ Slingback, Bootlick and Footpad
  - ❇ Serena, Instep and The Kitten Heels
  - ❇ Flipflop and Elves followed by Magigayle and Toecap
  - ❇ Stefan and Sue

WHO DOES WHAT?
(Let's Talk Business – and do some fun(d) raising!)

THE AUTHORS Firstly, a vote of thanks. Music theatre writers (that's us!) are creative business people who earn their living from royalties and performances, so many thanks for buying our book and CD and for paying the licence fee to cover performing rights to stage this **CLASS ACT PRODUCTION**. The licence also covers all copyright legalities, so you are free to photocopy our work.

We hope you enjoy staging the musical as much as we enjoyed writing it. For a free ad for your show, news on schools around the world staging our musicals, reviews from children, feedback from teachers and shared production ideas and tips, visit the Sara and Gavin website, http://www.writersofnote.co.uk.

THE PUBLISHERS International Music Publications edit, print and distribute our books and CDs. If you need extra copies, your local music shop can order them for you in no time. For a list of music shops in your area, see the back of IMP's Music at School catalogue or the How To Order page on IMP's education website http://www.music-at-school.co.uk. This excellent site has more information on this show and our other productions, usefully including sample pages to view. IMP also issue those licences mentioned above. Call +44 (0) 20 8222 9222 if you have any queries.

THE IMPRESARIOS (that's you and your team). We've written **CLASS ACT PRODUCTIONS** to be staged very simply, but because we appreciate that there are always expenses involved in putting on a show, we've developed a plan to help you recoup your costs (and even make a profit). Why not stage this show as a business, starting with an **ELVES AND THE SHOEMAKER** Sunday?

THE BENEFITS

Selling tickets for school shows may be something you haven't done before, but we've never met a parent yet who begrudged a small sum to see their child excel whilst helping their school raise funds for books, equipment, repairs, trips or whatever needs are most pressing.

It's a great way to support the school; the children learn from being involved in a commercial enterprise; it gives friends, parents and other family members an opportunity to take part in a school project; it involves the local community and you may even unearth a theatrical 'Angel' to sponsor the entire show (or see below for budget ideas).

Even if parents can only spare an hour, they'll be involved, especially if work commitments prevent them from coming to school during the week. It's worth a try. It builds pride in the school and its achievements; it's fun and it gives the best 'persuader' on the staff an ideal opportunity to press-gang er, encourage parents to help with the actual performance!

PRE-PRODUCTION

Give one class the project of designing a brief questionnaire to send to family members asking what skills and time they can contribute – it might be a surprise to find how much talent mums, dads, grandparents, older sisters and brothers can muster between them! Then hold your *ELVES AND THE SHOEMAKER* Sunday and invite volunteers along. Divide tasks by appointing Team Leaders for specific areas:

PRODUCER
* The person with overall responsibility for the show; the one who brings everything together. One of your first considerations may be money. Set a budget, divide it into manageable parcels and decide who might sponsor what:
* Costume (charity shops for winter outfits, old curtains for royal robes?)
* Scenery (will school Friends contribute paint, wood, hardboard, card, design ability?)
* Music (will one of the Governors cover the performance licence fee?)
* Face Paints (perhaps your local art and craft shop might oblige?)
* Approach your local drama group, college, operatic society or theatre (and beg) for help with costumes, face-painting, lights.

PUBLICITY MANAGER
* Unwrap IMP's complimentary Publicity Pack, despatched as soon as your performance licence fee is received. This invaluable resource is a bumper collection of goodies including colour copies of the book cover as posters and flyers, logos to photocopy and scan, badges to make and Sara and Gavin's Showbiz Tips.
* Run an inter-class competition to design the programme cover. The children can scan in any imagery from the Publicity Pack. Why not use the winning entry as your school Christmas cards to sell at performances to boost funds?
* Link this to a ticket and poster designing competition. Make the local community aware of what you're trying to do. Contact shops, sports centres or clubs to see if they'll sell tickets or display a poster (but if you put posters up at the roadside, get permission from your local Highways Department).
* Designate one group to write a press release, contact local newspapers and radio stations for publicity and organise a press photographer to take pictures at dress rehearsal.

ADVERTISING REPRESENTATIVE
* Motivate a group to sell prime space in the programme to local companies, school suppliers, parent-run businesses (even a business card on a quarter page of A5 for a small charge will help). They could e-mail one of the London theatres explaining their project and ask for a programme to see how the professionals do it. Visit www.writersofnote.co.uk for links to The Society of London Theatre and The Stage magazine.
* Approach a local restaurant about after-theatre suppers; see if the local college would like to advertise media courses; go to the top and ask the Chairman of the biggest local company or bank to place an ad.
* Use one of your IT lessons to post info about the show on bulletin boards on schools-related internet sites.
* Send saraandgavin@writersofnote.co.uk an e-mail 'plug' for your show.

PROGRAMME EDITOR

❋ Energise the programme with mini-interviews of your principal players, rehearsal reports, photos, *ELVES AND THE SHOEMAKER* poems, production team profiles, thanks to helpers, letter from the Head.

❋ For audience participation, print the story of *THE ELVES AND THE SHOEMAKER* and *MAGIGAYLE'S MUSICAL SPELL* in the programme, then sell it for a small charge in the foyer as your eager audience swarm in to see the show.

THEATRE MANAGER

❋ Allocate front-of-house duties. Appoint ushers to show guests to their seats. Older brothers and sisters might like to dress up for the role, bow ties included. Organise a lucky ticket draw or raffle with donated prizes. Sell refreshments. Ask a local supermarket or school catering supplier for free products to boost your profits.

STAGE MANAGER

❋ Appoint a backstage crew of Props, Scenery Painters, Set Designer, Prompt, Lighting, Stagehands. Dress your crew all in black like the professionals.

WARDROBE MANAGER

❋ Make one classroom into the Wardrobe Department on your *ELVES AND THE SHOEMAKER* Sunday by asking anyone who can drive a sewing machine to bring their machine and an extension lead and form a team.

CRECHE MANAGER

❋ Set up a play area for younger brothers and sisters – the pupils of tomorrow.

NOT LONG TO GO ...

❋ Don't worry if the dress rehearsal is disastrous. You know what they say – it'll be alright on the night!

❋ Check our Who's Done What? table as Opening Night draws near ...

IT'S SHOWTIME!

❋ Give the whole team a hugely encouraging pep talk before curtain-up (then get someone to do the same for you).

❋ Relax and enjoy the performance. The children will be wonderful and the audience will love it, even if something goes wrong, so stop worrying. You've done all you can. Hey, where are you going in that false beard?

AND AFTERWARDS?

❋ Go backstage and congratulate everyone in true theatrical style. Accept the bouquets, cheers and compliments with aplomb.

❋ Celebrate, go home, have a long hot bath and a long cool drink. Start planning next year's *CLASS ACT PRODUCTION* (maybe our nativity, *THE SHINIEST STAR*) whilst euphoria rules!

WHO'S DONE WHAT?
(Producer's Checklist)

TASK	WHO'S RESPONSIBLE?	✔
Has the Publicity Pack been received from IMP?		
Publicity campaign up and running?		
All roles cast? Even the smallest line or non-speaking part designated?		
Ensembles understand if they're Group 1 or 2?		
Percussion ready to beat, bash and crash?		
Backstage crew all set?		
Costumes all organised?		
Has everyone got their props?		
Has the performance licence fee been paid?		
Who's putting the chairs out for the audience?		
Programme ready?		
Programme sellers appointed and briefed?		
VIPs invited?		
Photographer booked?		
Scenery complete?		
Who's in charge of children backstage?		
Lighting organised?		
Ushers appointed?		
Raffle ready?		
Refreshments organised?		
Make-up/face painter prepared?		
Orchestra/pianist/CD player ready?		
Is the cast sure of the walkdown order for the Bows?		
Does everyone know the finale?		
Champagne on ice?		
Gifts/flowers organised for those who deserve them most (like you!)		
(And in case there's anything else we've forgotten …)		

THE STORY OF THE ELVES AND THE SHOEMAKER

Dear Audience
please join in!

NARRATOR 1	Hello everyone. Welcome to .... School.
NARRATOR 2	Please will you help us with our magical Christmas musical?
NARRATOR 3	When you see the word EVERYONE, say the song titles with us, like this:
EVERYONE	*IT'S HOLIDAY TIME!*
NARRATOR 4	*(to other Narrators)* I couldn't hear them. Could you?
NARRATORS	No!
NARRATOR 4	*(to audience)* Come on, you can do better than that. Ready?
EVERYONE	*(shouted) IT'S HOLIDAY TIME!*
NARRATOR 4	One more time
EVERYONE	*(louder) IT'S HOLIDAY TIME!*
NARRATOR 1	Thank you. Now we'll begin our story. In the snowy mountain village of Leather Uppers lives a poor shoemaker.
NARRATOR 2	His name is Stefan Sole
NARRATOR 3	and once he'd been rich and famous
NARRATOR 4	but because he's growing old and can't see very well, it takes him a long time to make his shoes,
NARRATOR 1	so he's no longer rich
NARRATOR 2	and he's no longer famous,
NARRATOR 3	but we'll tell you more about him when the town crier,
EVERYONE	*(loudly) TOECAP'S TALKING.*
NARRATOR 4	Once upon a time, the richest kings and queens in the world came here to buy Stefan's
EVERYONE	*(shout) SHOES*
NARRATOR 1	but now, *nobody* comes any more
NARRATOR 2	and that makes Stefan's wife, Sue, very sad, so she sings
EVERYONE	*(sadly) SUE'S LAMENT.*
NARRATOR 3	Then mean old Slingback, Stefan's evil landlord, who doesn't care about anyone or anything
NARRATOR 4	except money –
NARRATOR 1	– that's right – comes creeping round and tells Stefan, I'm
EVERYONE	*(wickedly) RAISING YOUR RENT.*
NARRATOR 2	This makes Sue even more sad and again she sings
EVERYONE	*(even more sadly) SUE'S LAMENT.*
NARRATOR 3	But then an amazing thing happens ...

NARRATOR 4	By magic, secret helpers arrive in the night to make the most fantastic shoes for Stefan and Sue and while they work, they sing
EVERYONE	*(short shouts)* **ELVES RAP**
NARRATOR 1	but you won't be able to see them until
EVERYONE	*(with amazement)* **MAGIGAYLE'S MUSICAL SPELL**.
NARRATOR 2	So, there's a really big surprise for the old shoemaker and his wife as
EVERYONE	*(with yawns)* **MORNING'S DAWNING**.
NARRATOR 3	Then we'll meet the incredibly glamorous
EVERYONE	*(slinkily)* **SERENA STILETTO**
NARRATOR 4	and by this time, Stefan and Sue think it's their
EVERYONE	*(joyfully)* **LUCKY DAY**.
NARRATOR 1	But the secret helpers haven't finished yet, so the
EVERYONE	*(more short shouts)* **ELVES RAP AGAIN**
NARRATOR 2	but you *still* can't see them until
EVERYONE	*(with wonderment)* **MAGIGAYLE'S MUSICAL SPELL**
NARRATOR 3	and then the village is full of Christmas shoppers who've come to
EVERYONE	*(greedily)* **BUY, BUY, BUY!**
NARRATOR 4	Next, fantastic news! The rich kings and queens come back because
EVERYONE	*(as a town crier)* **TOECAP'S TALKING SHOES**
NARRATOR 1	but the secret helpers *still* haven't finished, so the
EVERYONE	*(even more short shouts)* **ELVES RAP AGAIN**
NARRATOR 2	and Stefan and Sue make lovely presents for the elves because
EVERYONE	*(kindly)* **WHEN SOMEONE'S KIND**
NARRATOR 3	you thank them, that's what you do.
NARRATOR 4	Then everyone joins the celebrations because
EVERYONE	*(festively)* **IT'S HOLIDAY TIME!**

1 – IT'S HOLIDAY TIME!

(One child runs onstage)

SOLO VOICE   *(spoken)* It's snowing!

(More children run on)

TWO VOICES   *(louder)* It's snowing!

(Enter Toecap the Town Crier, followed by Ensemble, including Grandma and a bearded Grandpa who sit down on chairs at the side of the stage)

TOECAP   *(spoken)* Ladies and gentlemen,
.... School proudly presents
a *CLASS ACT PRODUCTION* of *THE ELVES AND THE SHOEMAKER!*

ENSEMBLE   School is all over now, holidays are here.
School is all over now, holidays are here.
Out to play every day, hear the church bells chime.
Skating on the lake, it's holiday time.

(During the next section, Naughty Boy pulls faces at his sister, Naughty Girl. She sticks her tongue out at him until the two groups notice their antics and Toecap growls at them)

GROUP 1	It's holiday time,
GROUP 2	it's holiday time,
ENSEMBLE	it's holiday time.
GROUP 1	Be nice to your sister,
GROUP 2	be nice to your brother,

TOECAP   *(growled)* be NICE!

(Naughty Boy jumps out from the Ensemble, scares Grandma and is told off by Group 1. Naughty Girl creeps up on Grandpa, who's dozing in his chair. Naughty Girl is just about to pull Grandpa's beard when Group 2 sing their warning line, followed by Toecap's second admonishment)

ENSEMBLE   Be nice to your grandma, it's holiday time.
Be nice to your grandpa, it's holiday time.
Be nice to each other, it's holiday time.
Be nice, be nice, be nice, be nice,

TOECAP   *(roared)* be NICE!

(Naughty Boy and Girl stand up straight this time. Toecap keeps his eye on them)

ENSEMBLE   Christmas is here, it's our favourite time of year.
                   We're going sledging, can anybody steer?
                   Climbing the mountain to hear the church bells chime.
                   Ding, dong, ding, dong.

GROUP 1   Holiday time,

GROUP 2   holiday time.

ENSEMBLE   Time to have fun and time to be kind.
                   It's Christmastime for everyone,
                   Christmastime for everyone.
                   Christmas, it's holiday time.
                   Christmas, it's holiday time.
                   Christmas, it's holiday time.
                   Shout it out, it's Christmastime!

ENSEMBLE	**DESCANT SINGERS**
Christmas, it's holiday time.	Ah.
Christmas, it's holiday time.	Ah.
Christmas, it's holiday time.	Ah.
Tell the world it's Christmastime.	Tell the world it's Christmastime.
Tell the world it's Christmastime.	Tell the world it's Christmastime.
Tell the world it's Christmastime!	Tell the world it's Christmastime!

2 – TOECAP'S TALKING

(Enter Toecap, followed by his sleepy apprentice town criers, Mutter and Mumble. Mutter carries a cushion bearing Toecap's handbell. Mumble carries a cushion with Toecap's tricorn hat on it. As Toecap opens his mouth, Mutter and Mumble speak first, which annoys Toecap)

MUTTER & MUMBLE   Hear, hear ye. Hear, hear ye.

(Toecap gestures to Mutter and Mumble for his bell and hat, then self-importantly rings his bell)

TOECAP   Welcome to Leather Uppers, the best shopping mall in the world. Right, Mutter?

(Toecap spins round to where he knows Mutter will be leaning against a yawning Mumble, just about to doze off. Mutter wakes up in a hurry and stands up straight)

MUTTER   Er, yes, right, Toecap.

(Toecap spins back round to address the audience. Mutter goes back to leaning on Mumble)

TOECAP   People from all over the world come here to spend their money. Right, Mumble?

(Mumble jumps to attention, trying hard to look awake as Toecap fixes him with a glare)

MUMBLE   Er, yes, right, Toecap.
TOECAP   Let's meet some of the shopkeepers.
MUTTER   The Candelabra
MUMBLE   family.

(Enter Benny and Barbara Candelabra and their five children. Benny and Barbara each carry a menorrah with one candle missing. Two of the children carry a candle each. The family line up across the stage, parent at each end)

BENNY   I'm Benjamin – you can call me Benny.
BARBARA   *(self-importantly)* I'm Barbara – you can call me *Mrs* Candelabra.

(The children pass a candle along the 'production line' to Benny until he has all the candles in his menorrah. Then they pass the other candle to Barbara until her menorrah is full)

BENNY   First I melt my wax, then I take my wick,
trim it, mould it, shape it, put it in my candlestick.

BARBARA   First I melt *my* wax, then I take *my* wick,
trim it, mould it, shape it, put it in *my* candlestick.

(Benny and Barbara hold up their menorrah up for the audience to see. Barbara checks to see how high Benny's holding his menorrah and holds hers higher)

BENNY & BARBARA   *(competitively)* Our menorrah, ready now for sale.

(Toecap steps forward, blithely blocking Barbara. Enter Donald Rump. He's a small , strutting man and on his arm is his glamorous girlfriend, Philly Meenyon, who's much taller than him)

TOECAP	Let's meet some of the customers.
MUTTER	Texan beef baron Donald Rump
MUMBLE	and his lady-friend Philly Meenyon.
DONALD	Howdy, folks. Just flown in on my private jet
PHILLY	to do something fantastic to his plastic.

(He pulls a concertina of credit cards from his pocket which he allows to unfold until they reach the floor. Philly takes it from him and hides it skilfully in her handbag. She admires the menorrah)

DONALD   *(proudly)* I love my ranch, I love a steak for lunch,
a steak for breakfast and for tea.

PHILLY   *(winking at audience)* His credit's good in every neighbourhood,
so Donald's good enough for me.

DONALD	*(expansively)* We'll take
PHILLY	fifty,
DONALD & PHILLY	mail 'em right away. *(The Candelabra family look triumphant)*
TOECAP	And now let me introduce our local bakers,
MUTTER	the Seed
MUMBLE	family.

(Enter Sesame and Poppy Seed and their five children. Sesame and Poppy carry a tray of pastries each. Two of the children carry a sugar-shaker. They line up, parent at each end)

POPPY SEED	I'm Poppy Seed.
SESAME SEED	I'm Sesame Seed.
POPPY & SESAME	Welcome to our bakery.

(The Seed children pass one sugar-shaker along the line to Sesame, who shakes it over his pastries, then the other sugar-shaker the opposite way, to Poppy, who does the same)

SESAME   First I weigh my yeast, mix it with my flour,
baking pretzels, bagels, doughnuts, hour after hour.

POPPY   First I weigh my yeast, mix it with my flour,
baking pretzels, bagels, doughnuts, hour after hour.

22

(Sesame and Poppy step towards the audience, offering their pastries. Toecap licks his lips)

POPPY & SESAME   Soft, sweet strudel, ready now for sale.

(Enter Darlene Deep, tough Australian opal miner and her husband, Doug, a man of few words)

TOECAP	More customers! Australia's richest opal miner,
MUTTER	Darlene Deep
MUMBLE	and her husband Doug
MUTTER	Deep? *(Mutter giggles)*

DARLENE	G'day, come from Sydney, right Doug?
DOUG	Yep!
DARLENE	For the best cakes in the world, right Doug?
DOUG	Yep!
DARLENE	I love my mine because it's mine, all mine. Those opals all belong to me.
DOUG	Yep!
DARLENE	*(lip-lickingly)* Soft, sweet strudel, we'll take all you've got.
DOUG	Yep!

(This starts a buying and selling spree, with money frenziedly changing hands and everyone singing their lines in unison. Don't worry, it's meant to sound like cacophony!)

BENNY & BARBARA	First I melt my wax, then I take my wick, trim it, mould it, shape it, put it in my candlestick.	}
DONALD & PHILLY	Make that fifty, mail 'em right away.	} *(in unison)*
POPPY & SESAME	First I weigh my yeast, mix it with my flour, baking pretzels, bagels, doughnuts, hour after hour.	}
DARLENE	Soft, sweet strudel, we'll take all you've got.	}
DOUG	Yep!	

(Enter Stefan, observing the happiness and prosperity).

DONALD		}
PHILLY	WHO'S THAT?	} *(in unison)*
DARLENE		}

(Buyers and sellers freeze. Stefan, poor and currently unsuccessful, is not welcome)

TOECAP	*(dismissively)* Oh, that's only Stefan Sole, the old shoemaker. They say he used to make wonderful shoes – once …

3 — SHOES

(Stefan takes centre stage He is stooped and looking old, struggling to make ends meet. He's cutting a piece of red leather to make what may be his last pair of shoes)

STEFAN
(sadly) Shoes, shoes, shoes, all my life was shoes, shoes, shoes.
Now no longer shoes, shoes, shoes, for I am too old to carry on.
Shoes, shoes, shoes, all I know is shoes, shoes, shoes.
What else can I do but shoes, for I am too tired to carry on.

(He brightens as he remembers how it used to be. He straightens his back, pulls back his shoulders and stands tall, reliving his past)

STEFAN
(proudly) Once when I was so much younger,
I made shoes with these two hands.
Shoes for rich men, pretty ladies,
kings and queens from far-off lands.

(A gong sounds. A fantasy sequence begins. Stefan is transformed. An assistant steps forward and helps him into a beautiful jacket and richly embroidered hat. Enter kings and queens, princes and princesses, all wanting Stefan's shoes. He tends to them all personally, bowing)

STEFAN
(enthusiastically) Yes, your majesty, no, your majesty,
yes, your majesty, no, your majesty!
Life was busy, hectic, fun, making shoes for everyone.

(The Shoe Parade of Stefan's designs takes place along a catwalk. These could be giant cardboard cut-out shoes carried by four Ensemble members as Stefan's staff. Ballerinas could display the dancing slippers and 'models', the fashion shoe)

TOECAP
(with gusto) The Everyday Shoe!
The Dancing Slipper!
The Fashion Shoe!

(The fantasy sequence and glamorous people exit. Stefan's hat is snatched off his head, his jacket torn off his back. His head droops as he leaves the red leather on his workbench)

STEFAN
(sadly) Shoes, shoes, shoes, all my life was shoes, shoes, shoes.
Now no longer shoes, shoes, shoes, for I am too old to carry on.

(Stefan despairingly puts his head in his heads, then sighs and starts locking up for the night)

4 – SUE'S LAMENT

(Enter Sue. Stage is low-lit. Sue has overheard her husband's sad words and sings privately to the audience as Stefan goes round locking up by torchlight)

SUE *(devotedly)* I can't weep 'til Stefan's sleeping,
never let him see my tears.
All these memories he's been keeping,
memories of his better years.

How could he work any harder?
What more could my man have done?
Empty purse and empty larder,
he believes he's let us down.

(FX: three loud knocks at the door. Evil Slingback and his nasty henchmen, Bootlick and Footpad can be seen at the window, sneering. Sue hides, knowing that Stefan wouldn't want her to witness a showdown with Slingback)

STEFAN *(with dread)* Slingback!

5 — RAISING YOUR RENT

(Enter Slingback, bullying property developer with wicked intentions. He is followed by his henchmen bailiffs, Bootlick and Footpad)

SLINGBACK	*(greedily)* I'm raising your rent again today. You're finding it harder and harder to pay, and as soon as you pay I'll put it up again next day.
BOOTLICK	*(stepping forward aggressively)* Yeah.
FOOTPAD	*(clenching his fist)* Yeah.
SLINGBACK	*(arrogantly)* Yeah.

(Bootlick and Footpad are thoroughly enjoying themselves, bullying Stefan from behind their boss. How brave would they be if Slingback wasn't there?)

BOOTLICK	*(with evil relish)* He's raising your rent again today.
FOOTPAD	*(mockingly)* You're finding it harder and harder to pay,
BOOTLICK	and as soon as you pay he'll put it up again next day.
STEFAN	I heard.
SLINGBACK	Pay me!
STEFAN	I can't.
BOOTLICK	Pay him!
STEFAN	I can't.
FOOTPAD	Pay him!
SLINGBACK	You will, I'll see to that! Come on, boys.
BOOTLICK	Ha!
FOOTPAD	Ha!
SLINGBACK	HA!

(Exit a sneering Slingback, followed by creepily fawning Bootlick and Footpad, impressed with their swaggering boss. Stefan, defeated, finishes locking up, sighing and shaking his head)

6 – SUE'S LAMENT (Reprise)

(Although she was hiding, Sue has overheard Slingback's threats and is desperately worried about Stefan. He exits, unaware that she was there. She steps forward to sing)

SUE

How could he work any harder?
What more could my man have done?

(Exit Sue. Blackout on stage as Sue's Lament ends. Into sparkly magical music for Elves. White Christmas lights onstage come on, then go off. Here's a chance to indulge in some magic. Objects may move e.g. pieces of leather on cotton threads being pulled across the stage or cardboard cotton reels being lifted on black canes by an offstage member of the crew, but no-one can be seen on stage. These Elves are invisible – for now!)

7 – ELVES RAP

(Enter Elves under cover of blackout, led by Flipflop, Elf Leader, laziest boss in Elfdom. We can hear the Elves, but we can't see them. If it's easier for you, the Elves can sing this rap offstage, making a scampering entrance when Magigayle has worked her spell. The 3rd Elf starts a chant and the others join in competitively, each trying to drown out their fellow Elves)

FLIPFLOP	*(bossily)* Come on, let's get started, we've got work to do.
1ST ELF	*(shouted)* I've lost my scissors!
2ND ELF	*(shouted)* Who's got my pins?
3RD ELF	Stitchin' it, sewin' it, gonna put a bow on it.
3RD ELF }	Stitchin' it, sewin' it, gonna put a bow on it.
4TH ELF }	Box of buckles, bag of bows.
3RD ELF }	Stitchin' it, sewin' it, gonna put a bow on it.
4TH ELF }	Box of buckles, bag of bows.
5TH ELF }	Lovely bit o' leather, stand the winter weather.
3RD ELF }	Stitchin' it, sewin' it, gonna put a bow on it.
4TH ELF }	Box of buckles, bag of bows.
5TH ELF }	Lovely bit o' leather, stand the winter weather.
6TH ELF }	Spit on it, polish it, got to get a shine on it.

(This becomes competitive cacophony. Enter the fairy, Magigayle to restore order. She could enter at the back of the hall, shout 'Stop!' from there, then walk down the aisle, through the audience, taking centre stage to work her magical musical spell)

MAGIGAYLE	*(shouted)* STOP!

(Elves are instantly silenced)

1ST ELF	Sorry, Magigayle.
FLIPFLOP	*(scolding, to Elves)* So you should be.
	(to Magigayle) They're really, really sorry, Magigayle, all of them.
MAGIGAYLE	*(disbelievingly)* Hmmm.
	(to audience) Of course, you can't see them, can you?
	Oh, we'll soon put that right.

8 – MAGIGAYLE'S MUSICAL SPELL

(Magigayle teaches the audience a spell to make the Elves visible. They may not be very good at this tongue-twister, but that's all part of the fun! Magigayle conducts the audience with her wand)

MAGIGAYLE	Repeat after me! The magical musical spell. Your turn!
AUDIENCE	The magical musical spell.
MAGIGAYLE	The magical musical, musical magical, magical musical spell. *(shouted)* Come on!
AUDIENCE	The magical musical, musical magical, magical musical spell.
MAGIGAYLE	*(in schoolmarmish style, 'writing' with the end of her wand)* Oh dear, oh dear, must try harder! You'll never see them if you sing like that. This time give it all you've got! After me! The magical musical, musical magical, magical musical spell.
AUDIENCE	The magical musical, musical magical, magical musical spell.

(The lights go up, the Elves appear from their hiding places and take up their sewing actions)

MAGIGAYLE	That's better, look, there they are!

(Elves are working hard, making shoes from Stefan's red leather, except Flipflop, who's sitting down, feet up, reading the Daily Elfegraph or Herald Elfbune. Magigayle, her job done, exits)

ELVES	When you're a little green elf, life is tough. Life's very hard and life's very rough. You're workin' all night and you're workin' all day. That's an awful lot of work for a little bit of pay.
FLIPFLOP	*(looking round the right side of his paper)* Work, work,
ELVES	*(tiredly)* all night.
FLIPFLOP	*(looking round the left side of his paper)* Work, work,
ELVES	*(resentfully)* all day. Workin' all night, workin' all day.

3RD ELF	Stitchin' it, sewin' it, gonna put a bow on it.
3RD ELF }	Stitchin' it, sewin' it, gonna put a bow on it.
4TH ELF }	Box of buckles, bag of bows.
3RD ELF }	Stitchin' it, sewin' it, gonna put a bow on it.
4TH ELF }	Box of buckles, bag of bows.
5TH ELF }	Lovely bit o' leather, stand the winter weather.
3RD ELF }	Stitchin' it, sewin' it, gonna put a bow on it.
4TH ELF }	Box of buckles, bag of bows.
5TH ELF }	Lovely bit o' leather, stand the winter weather.
6TH ELF }	Spit on it, polish it, got to get a shine on it.
FLIPFLOP	*(looking round the right side of his paper)* Work, work,
ELVES	all night.
FLIPFLOP	*(looking round the left side of his paper)* Work, work,
ELVES	all day. Workin' all night, workin' all

(It's growing light. Flipflop hears Sue and Stefan upstairs, so it's time for the Elves to disappear)

FLIPFLOP	Shh!

(Flipflop stands up and stretches, sleepily ready to lead them away. Elves put down needles and tiptoe offstage with Flipflop lazily beckoning them to hurry up)

9 – MORNING'S DAWNING

(Enter Stefan, stretching and yawning, unlocking doors and opening curtains to let in the daylight, which reveals, to his astonishment, the fabulous red shoes the elves have made)

STEFAN   *(an amazed shout)* Sue! Sue!

(Stefan shakes his head, walks around his workbench and looks around the room for any sign of someone to thank for this miracle. Enter Sue. Stefan shows her the shoes)

STEFAN   Shoes, shoes, shoes, never seen such shoes.

(Sue is stunned, delighted and touched that someone should do so much to help them. She quickly realises how much money the shoes will fetch)

SUE   Who would help us?
                          Who would do this?
                          Could this be our lucky day?

(She sees a customer approaching the shop and calls to Stefan)

SUE   *(shouted)* Quickly, put them in the window.
                          Someone's coming!

10 – SERENA STILETTO

(Enter Serena Stiletto, one of life's customers. She's a little rich girl, she's loves the finer things of life and she's just got to have those shoes. She travels with her own backing group, The Kitten Heels, who make their entrance now, and Instep, her manservant and bodyguard who pays for everything and obeys her in silence. Instep enters and stands, arms folded, upstage from Serena)

SERENA STILETTO   They call me Serena Stiletto.
I started my life in the ghetto,
but I always knew I would leave,
you've got to have faith and believe in yourself.

THE KITTEN HEELS   You got to believe.
Oo oo wah.
Oo oo wah.

SERENA STILETTO	**THE KITTEN HEELS**
This	
girl's in the	Oo
world of high	oo
fashion,	oo
	wah.
and	
shoes are my	Oo
favourite	oo
passion.	oo
	wah.
I	
like 'em with	Oo
buckles and	oo
bows	oo
	wah.

(She spots the red shoes in Stefan's window, does a double-take and points to them)

SERENA STILETTO	**THE KITTEN HEELS**
and	
I like 'em	Oo
red just like	oo
those	oo
	ba ba ba ba bah.
over there.	

(The Kitten Heels point to the shoes)

>   **THE KITTEN HEELS**
>   She gotta have those.

SERENA STILETTO
These shoes are speakin' to me, girls.
I've just got to have 'em.

(Serena nonchalantly raises an arm and snaps her fingers, not bothering to look over her shoulder. She's confident that Instep will know what she wants of him. She carelessly kicks off the shoes she wore for her entrance, no longer interested in them now she's seen this fantastic new pair)

(Instep crosses to Stefan and Sue, takes out a large bankroll of notes, pays Sue generously for the shoes and brings them to Serena, kneeling to fit them on her feet)

SERENA STILETTO	**THE KITTEN HEELS**
I	
like 'em with	Oo
buckles and	oo
bows	oo
	wah.
and	
I like 'em	Oo
red just like	oo
those	oo
	ba ba ba ba bah.

(Serena points down to the red shoes she's wearing with the utmost panache)

SERENA STILETTO	**THE KITTEN HEELS**
on my feet.	
	She gotta have those!

(Exit Serena on Instep's arm, followed by The Kitten Heels, in single file, looking coolly over their shoulders at the audience)

11 – LUCKY DAY

(Sue and Stefan look delightedly at each other, marvelling at the money in their hands)

STEFAN   *(excitedly)* She liked them.

SUE   *(with wonderment)* She bought them.

STEFAN   *(louder)* She loved them.

SUE   *(shouted)* She *bought* them!

STEFAN & SUE   *(dancing round the stage)* This is our lucky day!

(Sue holds the money out to him, then takes one note which she puts in the pocket of her skirt)

SUE   *(laughing)* Go buy some more leather. You have shoes to make!

(Stefan puts money in his pocket and, standing straight and looking years younger, sets off to buy leather. Sue waves him goodbye. Enter Ensemble to celebrate his good luck and enjoy the festive season. Sue dances through the Ensemble, telling people of their good fortune. This song represents the passing of a day as Stefan races around, through the audience as well, to find the best leather he can buy for his money, arriving home in the evening)

ENSEMBLE   School is all over now, holidays are here.
                         School is all over now, holidays are here.
                         Out to play every day, hear the church bells chime.
                         Skating on the lake, it's holiday time.

(Ensemble disperse and exit as Stefan runs back home with his leather)

STEFAN   Sue, I've bought some leather, I've bought some leather!

(Stefan wants to work into the night. He cuts the leather for two pairs of shoes but Sue is anxious that he will tire himself)

SUE   *(gently)* Don't be late, you should be sleeping.
                         Time to pack your work away.

STEFAN   *(puzzled)* Who would help us?
                         Who would do this?

STEFAN & SUE   Could this be our lucky day?

(Sue persuades him to leave the leather on his bench and go to bed. Exit Sue and Stefan, leaving an empty stage. Lighting goes to blackout)

12 – ELVES RAP AGAIN

(Enter Flipflop and Elves under cover of darkness, ready to sew the night away)

FLIPFLOP	*(bossily)* Come on, let's get started, we've got more work to do.
1ST ELF	*(shouted)* I've lost my scissors!
2ND ELF	*(shouted)* Who's got my pins?
3RD ELF	Stitchin' it, sewin' it, gonna put a bow on it.
3RD ELF } 4TH ELF }	Stitchin' it, sewin' it, gonna put a bow on it. Box of buckles, bag of bows.
3RD ELF } 4TH ELF } 5TH ELF }	Stitchin' it, sewin' it, gonna put a bow on it. Box of buckles, bag of bows. Lovely bit o' leather, stand the winter weather.
3RD ELF } 4TH ELF } 5TH ELF } 6TH ELF }	Stitchin' it, sewin' it, gonna put a bow on it. Box of buckles, bag of bows. Lovely bit o' leather, stand the winter weather. Spit on it, polish it, got to get a shine on it.

(Competitive cacophony returns. Enter Magigayle to quell the unruly crew)

MAGIGAYLE	*(shouted)* STOP!

(Elves obey immediately)

1ST ELF	Sorry, Magigayle.
MAGIGAYLE	*(to audience)* Look, we've been here before. You all know what to do.

13 – MAGIGAYLE'S MUSICAL SPELL (Reprise)

MAGIGAYLE	After me! The magical musical, musical magical, magical musical spell. *(shouted)* Come on!
AUDIENCE	The magical musical, musical magical, magical musical spell.
MAGIGAYLE	*(as the Elves appear)* Not bad, look, there they are!

(Elves are working. Flipflop's reading The Sporting Elf. Magigayle smiles at the Elves, but sighs at lazy Flipflop. She points her wand at Flipflop and grins at the audience, tempted to use a magical transformation and turn him into a hard worker, but changing her mind, she shakes her head and exits)

ELVES	When you're a little green elf, life's a whirl. You never find time to meet a little green girl. You're workin' all night and you're workin' all day. That's an awful lot of work for a little bit of pay.
FLIPFLOP	*(looking over the top of his paper)* Work, work,
ELVES	all night.
FLIPFLOP	*(looking out from under his paper)* Work, work,
ELVES	all day. Workin' all night, workin' all day.
3RD ELF	Stitchin' it, sewin' it, gonna put a bow on it.
3RD ELF } **4TH ELF }**	Stitchin' it, sewin' it, gonna put a bow on it. Box of buckles, bag of bows.
3RD ELF } **4TH ELF }** **5TH ELF }**	Stitchin' it, sewin' it, gonna put a bow on it. Box of buckles, bag of bows. Lovely bit o' leather, stand the winter weather.
3RD ELF } **4TH ELF }** **5TH ELF }** **6TH ELF }**	Stitchin' it, sewin' it, gonna put a bow on it. Box of buckles, bag of bows. Lovely bit o' leather, stand the winter weather. Spit on it, polish it, got to get a shine on it.
FLIPFLOP	*(looking over the top of his paper)* Work, work,
ELVES	all night.
FLIPFLOP	*(looking out from under his paper)* Work, work,
ELVES	all day. Workin' all night, workin' all
FLIPFLOP	Shh! *(Exit Elves and Flipflop)*

14 – BUY, BUY, BUY!

(Enter Stefan, heading straight for his workbench. He can't believe his eyes when he spies two pairs of wonderful shoes sitting there)

STEFAN   *(loud shout)* Sue! Sue!

(Stefan examines the shoes, marvelling at the workmanship. Enter Sue)

STEFAN   Shoes, shoes, shoes, never seen such shoes.

(He hands a shoe to Sue. She's delighted but more and more mystified)

SUE   Who would help us?
                     Who would do this?
                     This must be our lucky day.

(She sees customers approaching and calls to Stefan)

SUE   *(shouted)* Quickly, put them in the window. Customers!

(Enter Philly and Donald, Doug and Darlene, still finding ways to spend their money. They crowd round Stefan's window, watching him place the two pairs of shoes there. Philly and Donald go into the shop. Philly produces Donald's credit cards from her handbag and passes one to Sue. Donald is about to say that twenty pairs would be sufficient, but Philly has other ideas)

DONALD   We'll take

PHILLY   fifty,

DONALD & PHILLY   mail 'em right away.

(Doug and Darlene go into the shop and examine the shoes)

DARLENE   Lovely leather, send 'em on today.

DOUG   Yep!

15 – TOECAP'S TALKING SHOES

(Enter Toecap, Mutter and Mumble. Again, as Toecap draws breath to speak, Mutter and Mumble interrupt him. Stefan is at his workbench, excitedly cutting out lots of pairs of shoes from stacks of leather and passing them to Sue. Finished shoes are ready in the window)

MUTTER & MUMBLE   Hear, hear ye. Hear, hear ye.

TOECAP   *(shouted)* The magic happened night after NIGHT!

(Enter royal customers eager to buy Stefan's shoes again)

TOECAP   *(with great aplomb)* Once again, Stefan is the greatest shoemaker in the world!

(Stefan is caught up in the busy whirl. Sue watches, delighted to see him so happy)

STEFAN   Yes, your majesty, no, your majesty,
yes, your majesty, no, your majesty!
Life is busy, hectic, fun, making shoes for everyone.

(Exit royal customers until Stefan and Sue are alone on stage again)

STEFAN   Shoes, shoes, shoes, all my life is shoes!

SUE   Shoes, shoes, shoes, all his life is shoes!

(Sue is struck by the thought that they still don't know who has made this possible)

SUE   WAIT!
We were poor and we were hungry.
Slingback nearly threw us out.
We don't know who's changed our lives.
We'll watch tonight, we must find out.

(Stefan nods in agreement. Stefan and Sue hide in the workroom as the stage darkens. Enter Flipflop and Elves under cover of darkness, ready to sew the night away)

16 – ELVES RAP AGAIN (Reprise)

FLIPFLOP	Come on, let's get started, we've got even more work to do.
1ST ELF	(shouted) I've lost my scissors!
2ND ELF	(shouted) Who's got my pins?
3RD ELF	Stitchin' it, sewin' it, gonna put a bow on it.
3RD ELF }	Stitchin' it, sewin' it, gonna put a bow on it.
4TH ELF }	Box of buckles, bag of bows.
3RD ELF }	Stitchin' it, sewin' it, gonna put a bow on it.
4TH ELF }	Box of buckles, bag of bows.
5TH ELF }	Lovely bit o' leather, stand the winter weather.
3RD ELF }	Stitchin' it, sewin' it, gonna put a bow on it.
4TH ELF }	Box of buckles, bag of bows.
5TH ELF }	Lovely bit o' leather, stand the winter weather.
6TH ELF }	Spit on it, polish it, got to get a shine on it.

(Goodness, those Elves are noisy tonight! Enter Magigayle)

MAGIGAYLE	(shouted) STOP! (Elves obey immediately)
1ST ELF	Sorry, Magigayle.
MAGIGAYLE	(to audience) Ready? Oh, don't worry, I'll do it! (waves her wand) There!

(Elves are working. Flipflop's reading the Elf Street Journal. Elves wave at Magigayle, who looks at her wand as if she's fighting to control it, like a divining rod. She looks at Flipflop and grins at the Elves, who nod furiously, willing her to put a spell on Flipflop, but she exits, still tempted)

ELVES	When you're a little green elf, life is tough.
	Life's very hard and life's very rough.
	You're workin' all night and you're workin' all day.
	That's an awful lot of work for a little bit of pay.
FLIPFLOP	(from behind his journal) Work, work,
ELVES	all night.
FLIPFLOP	Work, work,
ELVES	all day. Workin' all night, workin' all
FLIPFLOP	Shh!

(It's dawn. Exit Flipflop and Elves. Stefan and Sue emerge from their hiding place, amazed)

SUE	We must help them as they've helped us.
STEFAN	Give them gifts for all they've done.
SUE	Little mittens, little jackets,
STEFAN	tiny boots to keep them warm.

17 – WHEN SOMEONE'S KIND

ENSEMBLE | When someone's kind to you today,
be kind to someone else and say,
please take my help and pass it on
and day by day and one by one
we all become that someone helping someone,
and round and round that favour spins
'cause somebody was kind to you.
A good turn lands where it begins
'cause somebody was kind to you.

SUE | *(sewing a tiny jacket)* Stitchin' it, sewin' it, gonna put a bow on it.
STEFAN | *(making little boots)* Box of buckles, bag of bows.
SUE | Lovely bit o' leather, stand the winter weather.
STEFAN | Spit on it, polish it, got to get a shine on it.
ENSEMBLE | A good turn lands where it begins
'cause somebody was kind to you.

(It's evening. Stefan and Sue leave their gifts and hide. Enter Magigayle, Flipflop and Elves)

MAGIGAYLE | Shh! Shh!
FLIPFLOP | Come on, let's get started, there's probably loads to do.

(Suddenly, the Elves see the outfits left ready for them)

1ST ELF | Look!
2ND ELF | Look!
3RD ELF | Look!
4TH ELF | Look!
5TH ELF | Look!
6TH ELF | Clothes
ALL ELVES | for us!

(They pull on their new boots and jackets, jumping with excitement, to Stefan and Sue's delight)

ELVES | When you're a little green elf, life's a whirl.
We're all dressed up to meet a little green girl.
We'll party all night and party all day.

FLIPFLOP | *(pleading)* Do a little bit of work for a bigger bit of pay?

ELVES | *(ignoring him)* Dance, dance, all night.
Dance, dance, all day.
Dancin' all night, dancin' all day!

18 – IT'S HOLIDAY TIME! (Finale)

(Enter Ensemble and all other characters until the entire company is onstage and excitement mounts!)

ALL
School is all over now, holidays are here.
School is all over now, holidays are here.
Out to play every day, hear the church bells chime.
Skating on the lake, it's holiday time.

It's holiday time,
it's holiday time,
it's holiday time.
Be nice to your sister, be nice to your brother,
be nice to each other, it's holiday time.
Yes!

19 – BOWS

(Here comes the applause! Ensemble take a deep bow to music from IT'S HOLIDAY TIME!)

(Mutter and Mumble shamble downstage to their Hear, hear ye theme, then sing)

MUTTER & MUMBLE   Hear, hear ye. Hear, hear ye.

(The Candelabras bow to music from First I melt my wax ...)

(Donald and Philly bow to music from I love my ranch ...)

(The Seeds bow to music from First I weigh my yeast ...)

(Doug and Darlene bow to music from I love my mine ...)

(Kings and Queens and Entourage bow to the fanfare music from SHOES)

(Slingback, Bootlick and Footpad make their threatening way through to bow to music from RAISING YOUR RENT to a shower of hisses and boos from the company and the audience)

(Serena Stiletto, Instep and The Kitten Heels slink downstage to bow to their theme music and loud whistles from the company)

(Flipflop and the Elves bow, then Magigayle and Toecap, followed by Stefan and Sue, to cheers from the company)

(Everyone sings WHEN SOMEONE'S KIND as the closing number)

20 – WHEN SOMEONE'S KIND (Reprise)

ALL
When someone's kind to you today,
be kind to someone else and say,
please take my help and pass it on
and day by day and one by one
we all become that someone helping someone,
and round and round that favour spins
'cause somebody was kind to you.
A good turn lands where it begins
'cause somebody was kind to you.
A good turn lands where it begins
'cause somebody was kind to you!

(Everyone raises their arms or points to the audience at the end of the song. Then, as the applause reaches fever pitch, the cast bow together, then gesture to the Musical Director or Producer and team, who take a bow. Finally, leaving their audience wanting more, the entire company take a flourishing bow, everyone waves and exits)

THE END

Happy Christmas from Sara and Gavin!

The Elves and the Shoemaker

A Magical Christmas Musical

Words and Music by
Sara Ridgley & Gavin Mole

1 – IT'S HOLIDAY TIME

Christmas tempo

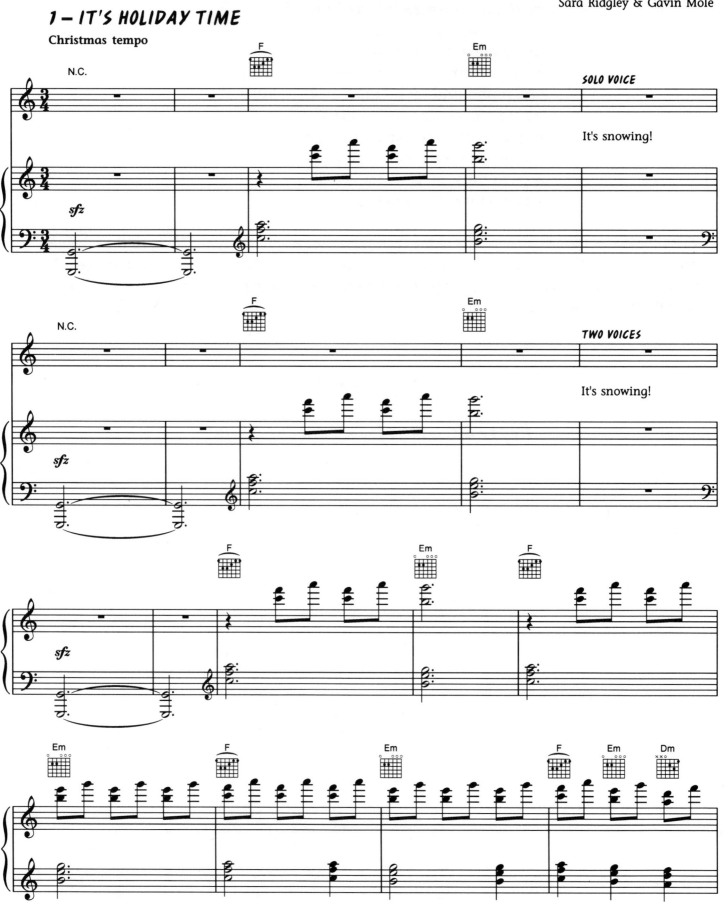

TOECAP

Ladies and gentlemen, ... School proudly presents a Class Act Production of 'The Elves and the Shoemaker'!

(gliss down)

ENSEMBLE

School is all o - ver now, ho - li - days are here. School is all o - ver now, ho - li - days are here.

2 – TOECAP'S TALKING

Talking tempo

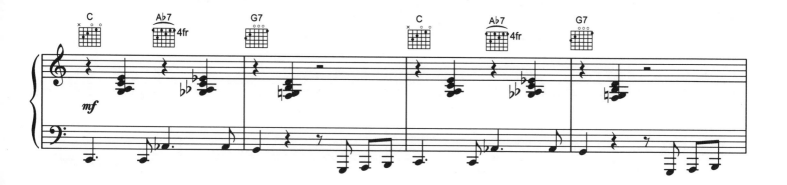

50

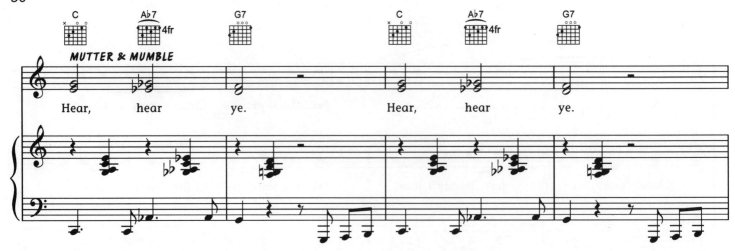

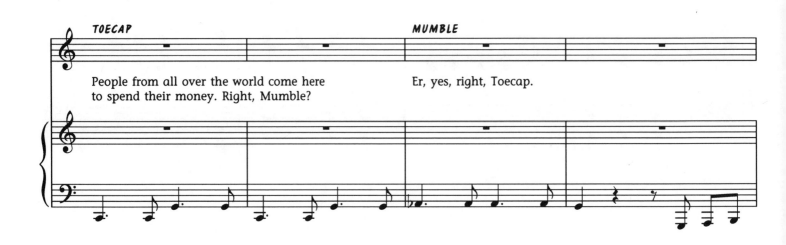

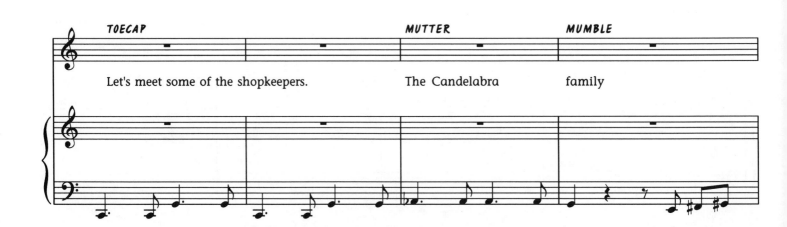

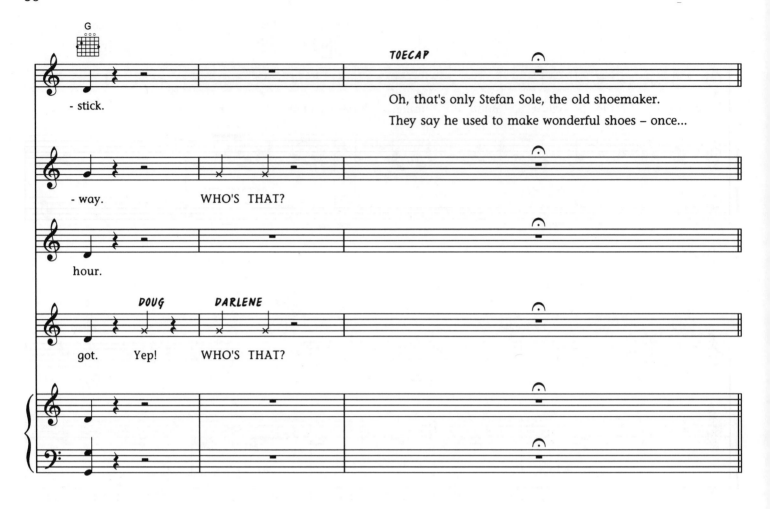

Oh, that's only Stefan Sole, the old shoemaker.
They say he used to make wonderful shoes – once...

- stick.

TOECAP

- way.   WHO'S THAT?

hour.

DOUG   DARLENE

got.   Yep!   WHO'S THAT?

3 – SHOES

Dejected tempo

STEFAN

Shoes,   shoes,

shoes,   all my life was shoes,   shoes,   shoes.   Now no lon-ger shoes,   shoes,

Slightly broader, regal

Life was bu - sy, hec - tic, fun,

mak - ing shoes for ev - 'ry - one.

SHOE PARADE

Everyday shoe tempo (faster)

TOECAP

The Everyday Shoe!

Dancing slipper tempo (slower)

TOECAP

The Dancing Slipper!

62

4 – SUE'S LAMENT

Devoted tempo

SUE

I can't weep 'til Ste-fan's sleep-ing, nev-er let him see my tears.

All these mem-'ries he's been keep-ing, mem-'ries of his bet-ter years.

How could he work a-ny hard-er? What more could my man have done?

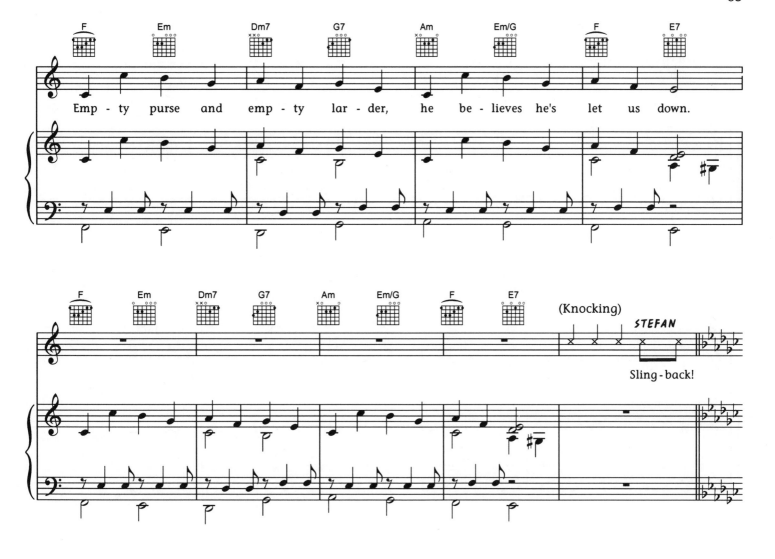

Emp - ty purse and emp - ty lar - der, he be - lieves he's let us down.

(Knocking)

STEFAN

Sling-back!

5 – RAISING YOUR RENT

Mean tempo

N.C.

SLINGBACK

I'm rais - ing your rent a -

p

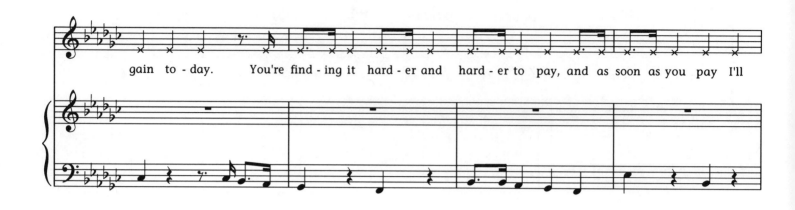

gain to-day. You're find-ing it hard-er and hard-er to pay, and as soon as you pay I'll

put it up a-gain next day. **BOOTLICK** Yeah. **FOOTPAD** Yeah.

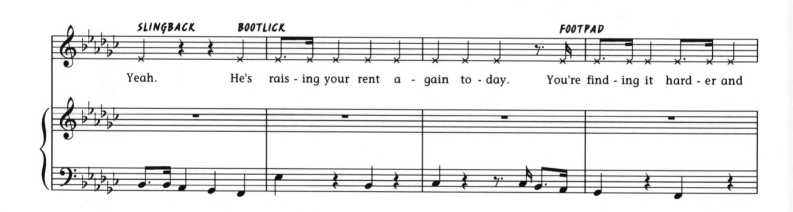

SLINGBACK Yeah. **BOOTLICK** He's rais-ing your rent a-gain to-day. **FOOTPAD** You're find-ing it hard-er and

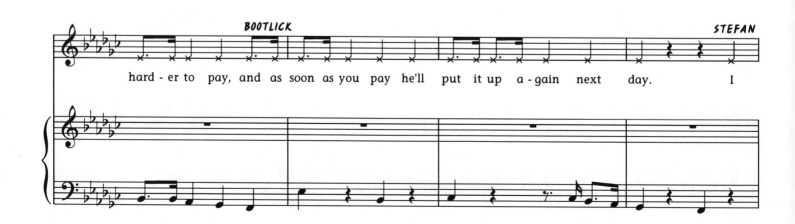

BOOTLICK hard-er to pay, and as soon as you pay he'll put it up a-gain next day. **STEFAN** I

6 – SUE'S LAMENT (Reprise)

Devoted tempo – again

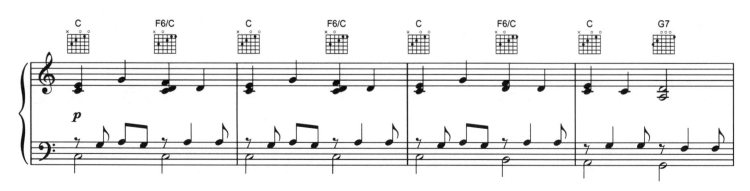

7 – ELVES RAP

Busy elves tempo

Come on, let's get started,
we've got work to do.

Stit - chin' it, sew - in' it, gon - na put a bow on it. STOP!

MAGIGAYLE

Box of buck - les, bag of bows.

Love - ly bit o' leath - er, stand the win - ter wea - ther.

6th ELF

Spit on it, pol - ish it, got to get a shine on it.

1st ELF

Sorry, Magigayle.

N.C.

FLIPFLOP

So you should be.
They're really, really sorry,
Magigayle, all of them.

MAGIGAYLE

Hmmm. (*to audience*) Of course, you can't
see them, can you? Oh, we'll soon put
that right.

8 – MAGIGAYLE'S MUSICAL SPELL

72

74

9 – MORNING'S DAWNING

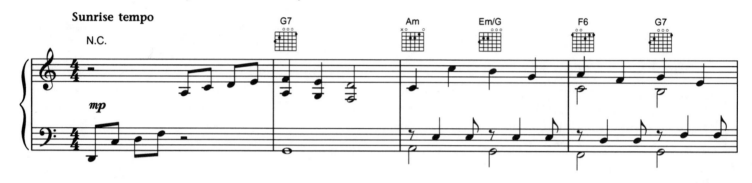

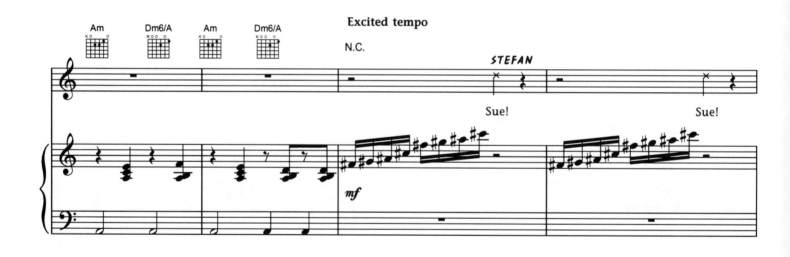

Shoes, shoes, shoes, ne-ver seen such shoes.

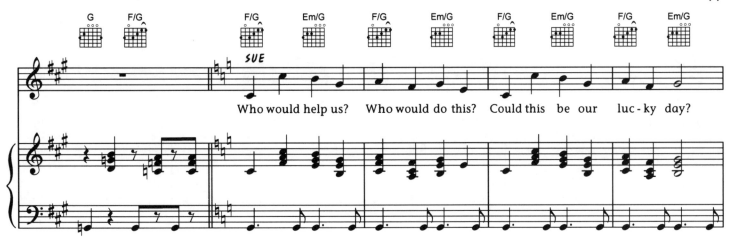

SUE

Who would help us? Who would do this? Could this be our luc-ky day?

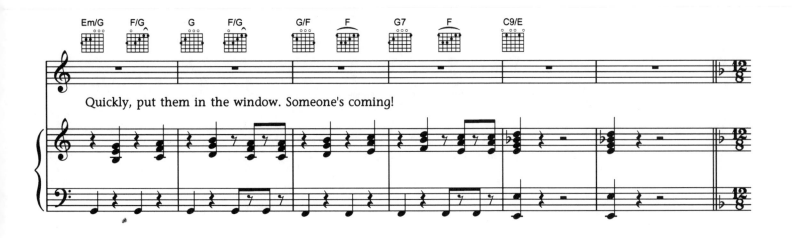

Quickly, put them in the window. Someone's coming!

10 – SERENA STILETTO

Slinky tempo

N.C.

mf

SERENA

They

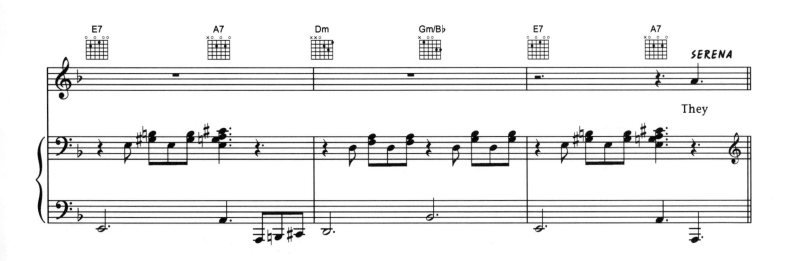

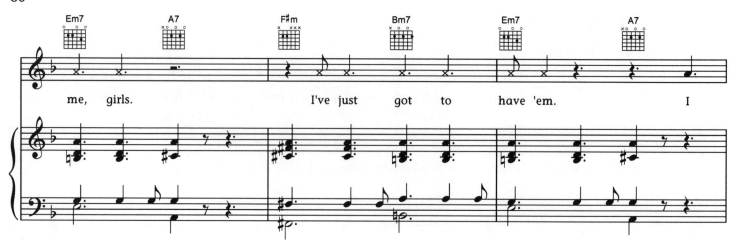

me, girls. I've just got to have 'em. I

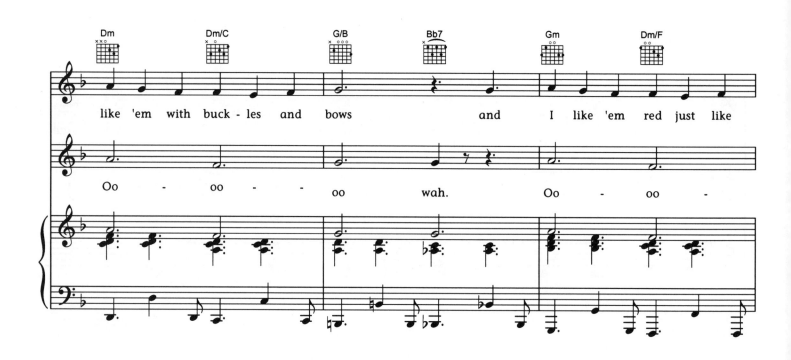

like 'em with buck - les and bows and I like 'em red just like

Oo - oo - oo wah. Oo - oo -

those on my feet.

oo ba ba ba ba bah. She got - ta have those!

11 – LUCKY DAY

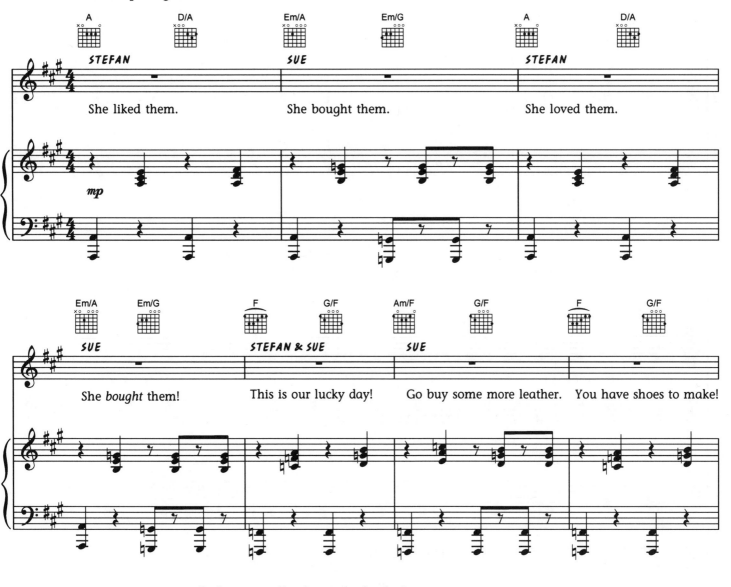

(Stefan runs off to buy some leather)

Playtime tempo

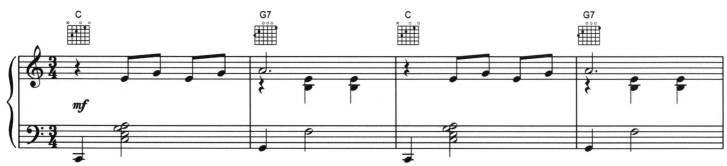

12 – ELVES RAP AGAIN

Busy elves tempo, again

FLIPFLOP

Come on, let's get started,
we've got more work to do.

1st ELF

I've lost my scissors!

2nd ELF

Who's got my pins?

3rd ELF

Stit - chin' it, sew - in' it, gon - na put a bow on it. Stit - chin' it, sew - in' it,

4th ELF

Box of buck - les,

13 – MAGIGAYLE'S MUSICAL SPELL (Reprise)

Magical tempo

14 – BUY, BUY, BUY!

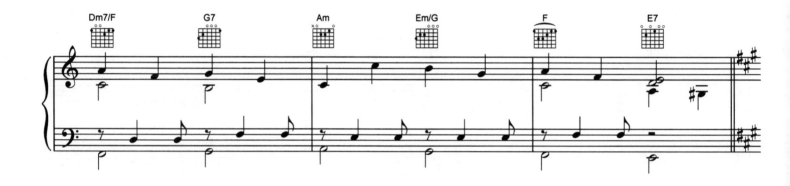

Even brighter

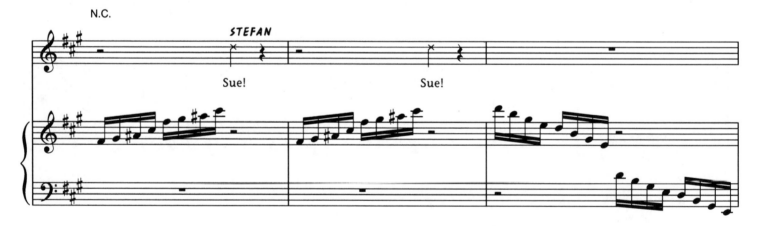

Brighter still!

Shoes, shoes, shoes, ne - ver seen such shoes.

92

15 – TOECAP'S TALKING SHOES

Town crier tempo

MUTTER & MUMBLE

Hear, hear ye. Hear, hear ye.

TOECAP

The magic happened night after NIGHT! Once again, Stefan is the greatest shoemaker in the world!

Regal tempo

GONG

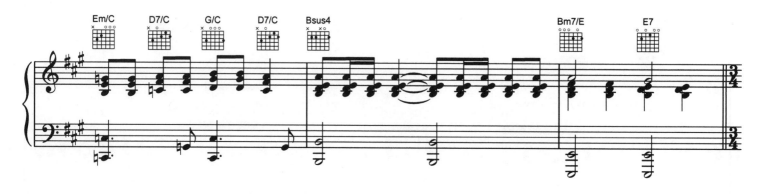

Happy waltz, one in a bar

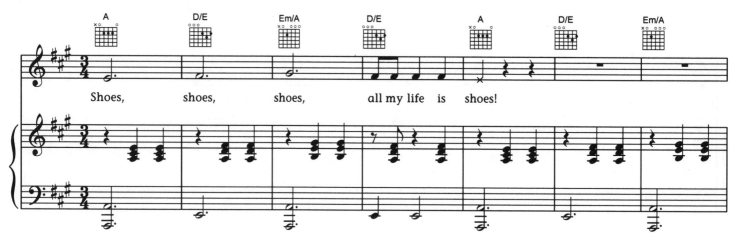

Shoes, shoes, shoes, all my life is shoes!

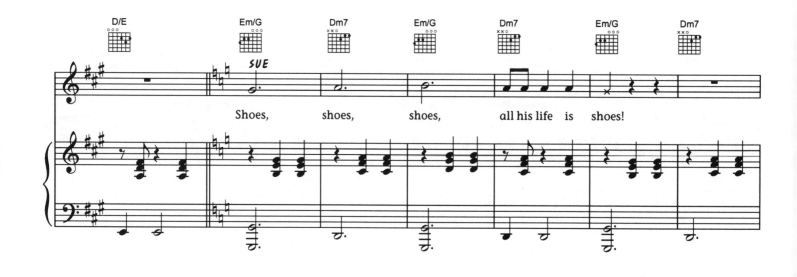

Shoes, shoes, shoes, all his life is shoes!

WAIT!

16 – ELVES RAP AGAIN (Reprise)

Busy elves tempo - again!

Come on, let's get started,
we've got even more work to do.

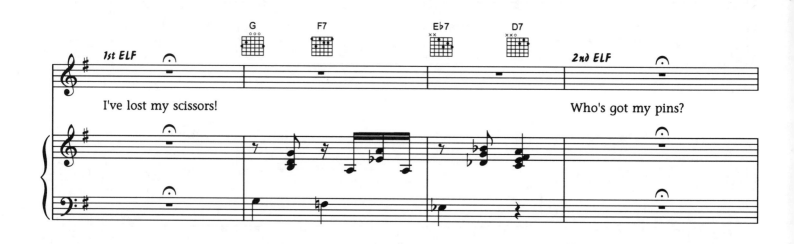

1st ELF
I've lost my scissors!

2nd ELF
Who's got my pins?

3rd ELF
Stit-chin' it, sew-in' it, gon-na put a bow on it. Stit-chin' it, sew-in' it,

4th ELF
Box of buck-les,

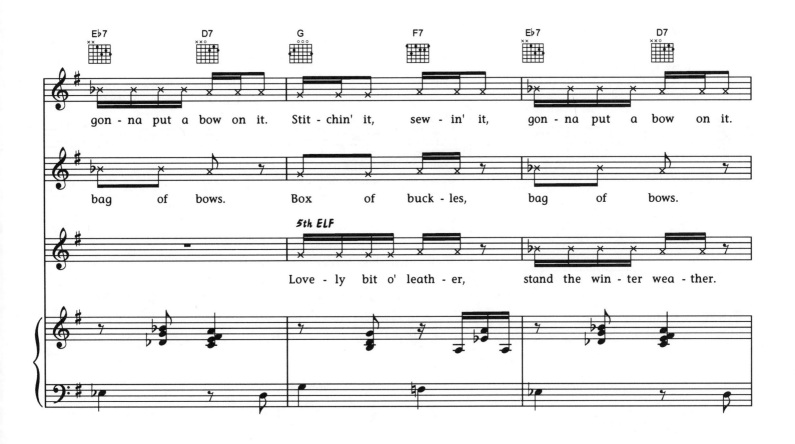

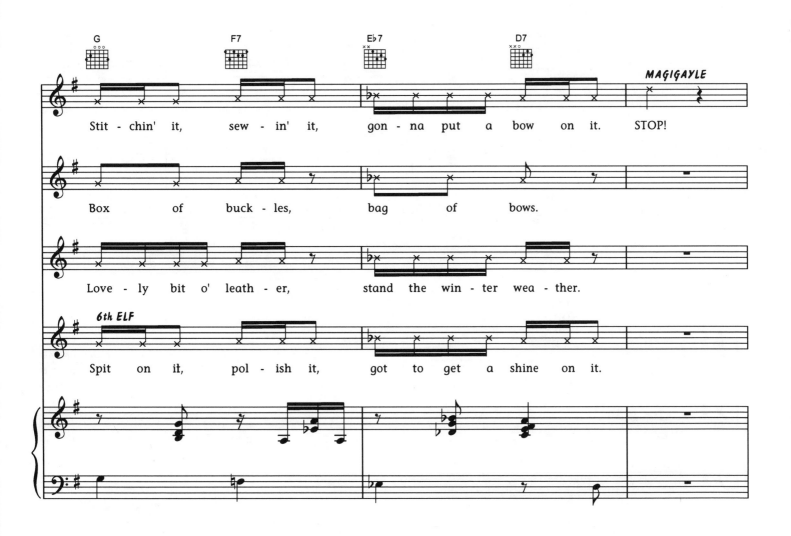

aw - ful lot of work for a lit - tle bit of pay.

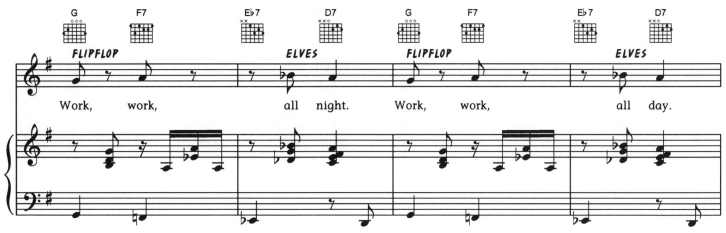

Work, work, all night. Work, work, all day.

Work - in' all night, work - in' all Shh!

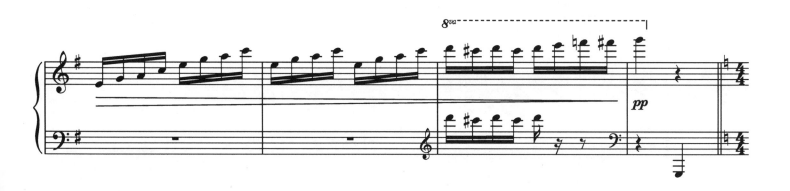

Thoughtful tempo

SUE: We must help them as they've helped us. STEFAN: Give them gifts for all they've done.

SUE: Lit - tle mit - tens, lit - tle jack - ets, STEFAN: ti - ny boots to keep them warm.

17 – WHEN SOMEONE'S KIND

Friendly tempo

ENSEMBLE: When some - one's kind to

G   F7   E♭7   D7   G   F7   E♭7   D7

SUE
STEFAN

Stit - chin' it, sew - in' it, gon - na put a bow on it. Box of buck - les, bag of bows.

G   F7   E♭7   D7   G   F7   E♭7   D7

SUE
STEFAN

Love - ly bit o' lea - ther, stand the win - ter wea - ther. Spit on it, pol - ish it, got to get a shine on it.

N.C.   F   Em   Dm7   G7

ENSEMBLE

A good turn lands where it be - gins_ 'cause some - bo - dy was kind to

C   F   C/E   Dm7   G7

MAGIGAYLE

you. Shh!   Shh!

18 – IT'S HOLIDAY TIME (Finale)

Holiday tempo

School is all o - ver now, ho - li - days are here. School is all

o - ver now, ho - li - days are here. Out to play ev - 'ry day,

nice to your sis - ter, be nice to your bro - ther, be nice to each

oth - er,   it's ho - - li - day

time. _____ Yes!

19 – BOWS

Christmas tempo

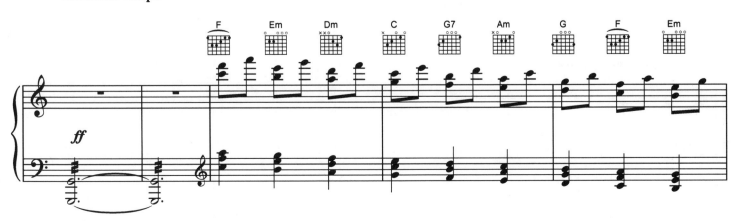

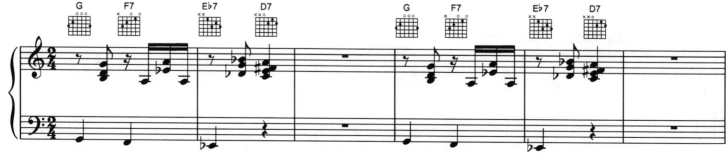

20 – WHEN SOMEONE'S KIND (Reprise)

Friendly tempo

When some-one's kind to you to-day,___ be kind to some-one

else and say,___ please take my help and pass it on___ and

day by day_ and one by one_ we all be-come that some-one help-ing some-one,___ and

CD TRACK LISTING

	Track Number Full version (with vocals)	Track Number Backing track (without vocals)	Length
It's Holiday Time!	1	21	3:22
Toecap's Talking	2	22	3:25
Shoes	3	23	3:31
Sue's Lament	4	24	1:03
Raising Your Rent	5	25	1:32
Sue's Lament (Reprise)	6	26	0:43
Elves Rap	7	27	0:49
Magigayle's Musical Spell	8	28	2:04
Morning's Dawning	9	29	0:44
Serena Stiletto	10	30	1:42
Lucky Day	11	31	1:39
Elves Rap Again	12	32	0:41
Magigayle's Musical Spell (Reprise)	13	33	1:32
Buy, Buy, Buy!	14	34	1:00
Toecap's Talking Shoes	15	35	1:59
Elves Rap Again (Reprise)	16	36	2:00
When Someone's Kind	17	37	2:41
It's Holiday Time! (Finale)	18	38	1:06
Bows	19	39	2:06
When Someone's Kind (Reprise)	20	40	1:09

Printed and bound in Great Britain 4/01

PERFORMANCE LICENCE FEE
APPLICATION FORM

If you decide to stage *THE ELVES AND THE SHOEMAKER*, you will require a Performance Licence. This licence covers the royalties due to the composers and publishers of the work and protects you and your school from any possible infringement of performing rights.

The average licence fee per musical ranges from £25 (excl. VAT) for the first performance and from £10 (excl. VAT) for each subsequent performance. The average licence fee for an individual song ranges from £10 (excl. VAT).

Please note: Blanket performance licences issued by the PRS or any other establishments *DO NOT* cover this work.

In return for your fee, IMP send you a free publicity pack containing Sara and Gavin's Showbiz Tips, colour posters, flyers, images to photocopy and scan, plus the Music At Schools catalogue.

Title of musical: *THE ELVES AND THE SHOEMAKER – A Magical Christmas Musical*

Composers: Sara Ridgley and Gavin Mole

Name of school: _____

Address: _____

Phone: _____   **Fax:** _____

e-mail: _____

Producer: _____

Other contact(s): _____

Number of performances: _____

Performance dates: _____

Are you recording the show?

Sound recording: Yes/No   No of copies: _____

Video recording: Yes/No   No of copies: _____

Please copy this form and send it to:
Copyright & Licensing Department
IMP Ltd
Griffin House
161 Hammersmith Road
London W6 8BS
Tel: 020 8222 9251
Fax: 020 8222 9264
e-mail: matt.smith@warnerchappell.com